PRAISE

A diary in verse, a collection of works that document a trip from near madness to a happier place. Although Ms. McPherson professes to not be a musician, she shapes her words like notes into a symphony of the senses, while engaging her thirst for knowledge and her wry sense of humor. Her descriptions of the music world are unequalled. Sandra is a rare talent and a good friend.

— Charlie Baty, guitarist of
Little Charlie and the Nightcats

ABOUT SANDRA MCPHERSON'S EARLIER WORK:

"a reckless, confident, and entirely personal idiom.... a hauntingly powerful voice. Her poetry comes out of what seems to be a very real turmoil of secret forces....an unignorable warmth, unflinching concern."

—James Dickey

"most of all—what Zeami called the 'flower' of art—surprise."

—Gary Snyder

"It's like turning the light switch off, and there in the dark—reality: all kinds of likely and unlikely things, incandescent on their own, beginning to stir and breathe."

—Elizabeth Bishop

"a master of the unexpected"

—Adrienne Rich

"a miner's eye for translucent color in the earth, and a painter's eye for the 'hard catchable light' in the air. Tough-minded and precise, she has a genius of an ear."

—Annie Dillard

SPEECH CRUSH

Published by Gunpowder Press
David Starkey, Editor
PO Box 60035
Santa Barbara, CA 93160-0035

Cover image: Katherine Ace, "Cinderella with Shoes."
Used with permission of the artist.

ISBN-13: 978-1-957062-04-4

www.gunpowderpress.com

SPEECH CRUSH

POEMS

SANDRA MCPHERSON

GUNPOWDER PRESS • SANTA BARBARA
2022

ACKNOWLEDGMENTS

I am grateful to the following publications for bringing these poems into print:

Agni: "Class Act / Art Class: Sutter Psych Hospital"

Basalt: "Upon Your DNA"; "The Larry Shirts"; "Mères à nu"; "Quicksilver, Cougars, and Quartz"

Brilliant Corners: "For Little Charlie & The Nightcats, on St. Cecilia's Day"

Cimarron: "My Birth Father's Pencil: Drawing of an Illusion of Wisdom"; and the SPRINGFORMS series: "Sonnet Composed in Disturbance", "Feeding the Giants", Thirstiness"; "Restraint"; "Egypt"

Crazyhorse: "Coupleting Discretely"; "Current, Matadero Creek"

Ecotone: "You Get a Free Shadow along with Me"

Epoch: "Foraging for Sound"; "Why I Won't Go Back to Hell"; "Double Elegy"

Field: "Runneth Over"; "Swimming During Polio"; "Letter Resembling Things"; "Hematological"

The Iowa Review: "Lute Frets Ghazal"

JAMA: "The Exact Shade of Code Grey: Sutter Psych Hospital"

Kenyon Review: "The Dijon Sky"; "My Daughter Visits Me at High Camp, Placer County, on My Fifty-Second Birthday"; "For Eleanor, from a Line by Zora Neale Hurston"

Michigan Quarterly Review: "Faith"

Nine Mile Magazine: "Henry, Praying: Sutter Psych Hospital"; "Mad Boy in the Odorscape: Sutter Psych Hospital"; "Women's Wing: Sutter Psych Hospital"; "A Quaver"; "Finishing"; "Names at Land's End"

Pedestal: "For Cindy, Who Cut Her Own Throat: Sutter Psych Hospital"

Ploughshares: "Courbet is a Desperate Man"; "After Trauma"

Plume: "Archaic Rayon Kamehameha"; "Dodge Ridge"; "Tenderly"

Poetry: " Last Conversations"; "Sitting on a Desk Together at SMU, 1982"; "Speech Crush"; "Las Hormigas"; "Said

the Parakeet"; "Investigation in Gray and Gaudy"; "New Friend"; "Spill"
Red Wheelbarrow: "Timing"
TriQuarterly: "Choro for a Father Dancing"; "The Senses"
Vox Populi: "Birth Mother,"
Willow Springs: "Simple Science"
The Yale Review: "Coördinates"; "Five Blind Boys"

"You Get a Free Shadow along with Me" was nominated by *Ecotone* for a Pushcart Prize; "Henry, Praying" was nominated by *Nine Mile Magazine*. "Timing" won the *Red Wheelbarrow* 2019 Poetry Prize. "Cinderella" appears in a slightly different form in *Patron Happiness* (Ecco Press, 1982).

My greatest thanks goes to Lee VanDemarr; Harold Louis Johnson; Henry Carlile; Susan Kelly-DeWitt; Alfred Corn; Malia McCarthy; and Randy White—for their empathy and aesthetic assistance. Claudia Mauro provided timely help. Bob Herz and Steve Kuusisto of Nine Mile Press rescued the Sutter Psych Hospital theme by publishing the entire work, *The 5150 Poems*, while freeing several of its character poems to integrate with the mental healthiness of *Speech Crush*. And, importantly, all my love goes to Joan Swift, to whose memory this book is dedicated.

Contents

"My soul is my weapon, I won't conceal it."

— Jarekus Singleton, "Refuse to Lose"

"You do not comprehend yourself
until someone steps to you,
grateful you are carrying that lantern."

— Laura Jensen

ONE

For Cindy, Who Cut Her Own Throat: Sutter Psych Hospital

You most reminded me of that young
rattler mid-trail in the hills—
its lax but ready body
measuring three-hundredths
of a mile, I guessed.
But barbed-wire's lace is the more obvious
likeness to your scars,
the fashion of them, their short slashes crossing,
with the look of something costly.

Still, a young snake's realistic—
it will grow, the knife-line life-drawing will heal.
You found a board and care;
that took a while but now it's responsible
to safe-keep and discharge you. You're scared
but better than when we met
four weeks ago. Tall and beautiful,
you show how thought has worn you.

You will not wear a turtleneck—
a paring knife of a ruffle
will always show.
And long-necked, not like a snake,
you're like a swan. A snake
makes it under the wire. A swan
swims, Cindy, in the blue holes of your eyes.

For Eleanor, from a Line by Zora Neale Hurston

I remember you,   your things,   you through your things.
Look: On your horizon a sugar-bowl is setting.
The sea is decorated by wind.
Pictures are up,   small as sponges.
One shelf at a time,   you extend yourself:
objects-in-waiting   for a lady.
She stood there until something fell off the shelf inside her.
Kutani dice cup,   Austrian butterfly pin-dish.

I think this through.   There's a void.   I have a sill.
There is a corner.   There's a piano top.
I look,   through yunomi and chalice,
through vase,   out the pane;   I window-shop
for the world she's in.   She knew to love things gingerly.
She'd roll each in her palms,   decode marks on the foot,
covertly rub rims for nicks and hairline cracks.

She stood there until something fell off the shelf inside her.
Look: A relish-turtle.   Celadon waterdropper.
Brown glaze fisherman,   boat caught in lotuses.

Something fell off.   And in my arms I caught her son.

Cinderella

When she came to the mirror it was to her
Instrument of change, every scene in it
Total background, and her hard looking
Asking only to be plumbed the depth
Of a diamond needle, the broken in her
Still breakable as if new. A red line rose
And fell between images of dawn
And sunset...

       This was the dream room,
That had been lived with and never opened.
Everything in it was imagined, the curtains
As seed-pearl as Li Qingzhao, with large printed
Purple blooms like distant ferris wheels
At dusk. At night the stars used themselves
Up on the rug.

       Footsteps sounded
Into many years. Now someone enters
By the window. She turns, quiet.
The temperature drops. On the sill she finds
The alchemical gold ginkgo leaf and it fits
Perfectly the foot that she puts down
Gently on the beginning of autumn.

The Senses

1

Sorted apart from the wise
by childhood, we played with an invention
that showed us two views of any hollow

will make it deeper. Aunts and uncles,
gone like winter warmth when the door opens,
lent us their stereoscope Sundays and slid

a box of scenes across the floor.
Our mouths still rang with the lemony sap of sourgrass
skirting the border between neighbors, between January, February.

Two flowers apiece
and the emptying bed began to show us its dimensions,
a quadrangle of earth, a trapdoor root-room.

Only when Ursula opened Poe to the *Pendulum*
did we put aside the stereoscope
and box of views, and spit out the stems.

We were always eager to listen
flat on our backs:
"I was sick—sick unto death with that long agony;

I felt that my senses were leaving me."
And on we read, letting a candle burn
until its pedestal began to bubble and fume,

our fingernails fidgeting across new bodies
of gooseflesh. Then we would hear it,
that "rich musical note,

the thought of what sweet rest there must be
in the grave." We hugged
the boards above the crawl-space;

we thought we'd never have the nerve to go down there

2

where it was true: Beneath
the white lips of Poe's black-robed judges
raising the syllables of our names

lay for each of us the future colored bridal dress,
its tinted veil, the surprising kiss
in a room with a cockatiel

whose colors ate away the cage.
For one morning of a later year,
at my wedding reception it dawned

what I'd been shivered by in our rites of Poe.
Above the coat-bed where I fished
for the roomy jacket of my maternity

bridal suit, an uncovered bird was wide awake.
It was as old then as I am this year
and spoke beautiful nonsense.

The invited couples, separated now,
were dancing fast, the houseplants tapping,
timidly cutting in. It already seemed very late

for marriage,
very much more like the withering hour
of parting. A snapping turtle gloomed away

from the bird's pearl face, mint crest.
When I touched my cousin Ursula,
matron of honor, to kiss her on the cheek,

her mouth's lavender—
the shade you can see now
if you can see what a mirror can't—

blazed on my lips.
(We hate white lips
and what is as rare as lipstick

in a judge's chambers?)
While the cockatiel snapped its bill, its judgments,
I threw the last of them away:

"Come to my senses!" I begged her again.

New Friend

I was making a new friend,
blonde-gray, a living opal,
pellucid, also reminding me
of a green apple
napping underneath its tree,
where I have tumbled too,
being of an age, "elderly"
but undepressed, she
tall enough to change
the smoke alarm,—sharing
a ripeness that we liked comparing,
bosses who couldn't see us,
perforation by divorce,
retirement and stairs.
One lunch that I was looking forward to
the first thing on her mind—
"Do you believe in the Occult?"—
"Merline! No, I don't think so."
She was in an auditorium—
her older, deader sister sat
right down beside her
with a message—a large figure
not her body but a sum—
what did it mean? I'd thought
one of us leaned forward at the lectern
but a ghost was there, holding sway,
or forth. Well, it came true—
she's richer by that sum—
and urges making sure
to be attentive to my dreams.

She knows that it will happen—
I'm her friend, as the Occult has been so far.
I didn't want my brother
appearing in a dream
to bring me news of unexpected
income—if only I would pray
about it first—to the God
who had my brother die
after all. And certainly not
my sister prophesying ill
on my behalf. I guess I'd stand up,
put on a mic, look out at all
the empty faces, make them
look alive, and even cheer.
Had I remembered a firsthand poltergeist,
a temptacious legend...
I guess I'd accept a sleek angora bunny
in a mohair hat, or magic
like a two-dollar bill, ask for
a life my brother could have back.

After Trauma

All I ever needed to bring up with her was cranberries.
She brightened no one's eyes; I befriended her frown.
Bogs, she says, when I rhyme *fog*.
Bone-chilling overcast, she affirms damply.
Wouldn't you like to slip away from your burned house
and head to the cold coast, even if they have to search
for you? I did that when the fire of marriage
scorched my heart. I hid in the low mist.
I was three months along and wanted to lie with the deer.
Mushroomy bottomland, its spires raised in purples and blues,
swamp ferns and skunk weed filled in with frogs.
Ditches soaked clean cattails muddy.
I used to wear a watch: if I wasn't found, I'd turn around.

Ravens flew to the corner of my eye like forests of winged ink.
I knew she felt their cinders too:
Though she was safe here, I saw her rise
out of her wheelchair and swing at the nurse.
An aide held me back. It shook me, but now
my violent friend sounds calmed, discussing cranberries.
Where all do they grow? Why don't we eat them always?
I want us to talk next of blackberries. But no, she says,
blueberries are next; they grow here too
and she can feel their essence, their gist, from long ago.
Blueberries it is; we're on a roll, our moods indigo.

Timing

When the positive came back, she had the prescription
in her purse. When that whole wondrous tiny head
of hair came out of there like a cub bear, she licked
its sweet cocoa fur. But after that, she *was* finally on
the pill when from an ill-lit corner of literature—it was
a woman's shelf, in a basement Berkeley bookstore—
she bought *Leaflets* to be signed in the future,
when her kid was grown, by motherly Adrienne—
strong inky-cap strokes, "With love." The pill-pack
wore lavender scrubs under foil. Dear Searle,
Djerassi, and Sanger, first there was fertile Nineteen
Sixty-six. But not before sex. Until, as the song goes,
there was you, Pill. Then the priest gave the girl hell,
so her glance, for love, swung back: "It makes me equal."

Coördinates

Zayante latitude 37° 02' 53" N, longitude 122° 04' 05" W
Bean latitude 37° 03' 05" N, longitude 122° 03' 41' W
Ferndell latitude 37° 03' 5" N, longitude 122° 05' 42" W

A favorite spot—and I could feel it barefoot—
The confluence of the Bean and the Zayante.

There was a third stream there—
A waterfall where Ferndell Springs

Jumped off. Why three?
Why not, the tipped earth said.

Downstream meant San Lorenzo.

And I could map it with my toes.

The three psychologies of water—
Stones, sand, and precipice.

There are more, of course. Sixteen,
When the woman

Of water comes of age.
Because that means a kiss, a pinch.

Just ask the crawdad,
And my conscious toes.

Hemetca mukurma, sii sayyan-ta—
One woman, water at the heel.

It was safe to go there
As a girl—or as Ohlone woman.

Hiked many times: that nexus
To her gravesite, lost

Now among the biggest sempervirens,
"The Neck-Breaker."

We were taken to its burly base, too big to be a foot
(The trees *did* have names),

Which wouldn't be incensed
If, in prayer, you didn't kneel...

With every stream I now expected to see the great
Rio Buenaventura; and Carson hurried eagerly to search...

The burned-out, burn-hearted, on-living tent
Of a surveyor's redwood

Pre-statehood that stood
In the right-of-way
Of the lengthy shortest flow from coast to coast.

Longitude 121° 49' 52"—
The maps continually veined it in their time.

Day after day—thinking he had found it
With every new stream until, like me he abandoned all idea

Of its existence...
Frémont and scouts camped there; inside the tree was coziest.

Later the cut-in domestic shelf.
Step-downs: tangible beaver cuttings, cartographers'

Mis-measurements, oh finally myth.
The dreaded *vast interior lake,*

Whose bitter waters brought us arid disappointment...
But, now, you can feel

Her knowing health, and when the time came
Who carried her to burial?

Long gray-haired rapids.
Each twist counted by a Being Everywhere.

Cool the fish-skin of your shins.
Climb up-canyon, arms through
Boughs, then grip
Flights of roots, those ancients, wrangling,

Young ones wriggling out of duffy mudstone
(As Mars, Earth's co-chair, has).

She was the single one.
Found herself this place: beach, fish, favorite acorns.

As in love, loosening its bindings, it happens
That in *place* somebody else comes along—

In this case
A learning little girl, her toughened feet.

Singing for spirits, playing fossil games...
Knitting, I'd squint up to the black-green-sungold

Knitted canopy, tell minnows from tadpoles, recount
Dogwood to madrone.
Peoples' pebbles. To be a pebble's person.

A favorite spot—and I could feel it barefoot—
The confluence of the Bean and the Zayante.

There was a third stream there,
A waterfall. Why three?

Doesn't everyone ask the crawdad?
Kuksu, the confluence murmured, purling over shells and sharks' teeth.

Last woman ever there.
Muwékma, la gente, the people.

A place-name for it?
"My fill of," said the place,
Never having had to have it.

Tenderly

(Mt. Hermon, 1961)

I played hymns, rhapsodies Hungarian and Blue.
Yet my "Tenderly" humiliated the evangelist.

When was it, months later? he told me I'd never get a job there.

That big old redwood hall came back as I practiced this morning.

I was the accompanist so couldn't play the melody line at the same time
Terry did. Just maybe when his sax laid out.

I can't remember if he sang a chorus in his Mel Tormé voice.

Fifty years later, he says we rehearsed just briefly enough to pull it off.

There were parts of my solo
That were not mistakes.

I started with its intro, backing in. Why don't poems do that more often?

Is a bridge never backwards?

And some listeners may have been moved by it, and relaxed, and tenderly
Touched one another. And the redwoods, which we save
In other ways, big things, found their innermost tender rings.

Ella Fitzgerald, Rosemary Clooney, Nat King Cole, Chet Baker, Louis Armstrong,
Tony Bennett, Miles, Ellington, Bill Evans, Johnny Mathis, Oscar Peterson,
Bud Powell, but not Terry and Sandy.

They had jobs—famous work—singing it.

The rest of the time the worshippers sang, "Softly and Tenderly Jesus is Calling."

My Birth Father's Pencil:
Drawing of an Illusion of Wisdom

My old hippie progenitor,
preferring binoculars for birds offshore
to mankind up-close,

heir of an artistic aunt with Carmel cottage
near Jeffers' Tor, among the cypresses
she sketched for postcards,

ran graphite in his bloodline, and
had printed on one of the six sides
of a hundred pencils

a motto all his own,
THE HUMAN RACE IS RUN AND LOST. We
still have some unsharpened.

With these in hand, no matter what
we were going to write,
the whole human race would be involved,

be at stake; though
we could count on how a pencil works
in a mundane dependable kind of way, if one was

a holy scribe or ransom-note drafter or
tosser of a stick for a retriever,
or empathetic with aspiring, fatalistic driftwood kindling.

Or like me, a poor housekeeper whose lead-soul woodgrain
pencil comes and goes from its drawer,
in spite of my preference for

that variant
with four colored rods
that rotated; or the black jumbo #1

the Haida totem carver used on his huge Seattle waterfront log,
his forested version of quarried marble,
to draw the curves of eyes and beaks and claws.

I even rather cherished the little ones
(in the hospital for minds gone wrong)
I fiddled with, too stubby

to be of harm to self and others,
or my good adoptive Dad's on the golf course,
busy keeping his skillful score.

Could a pencil stand for a bar set too high?
Or prop as low as the limbo dancer's close shave?
Any of us can master sleight-of-handwriting,

flip gradient, race across a page with that neutral shade of scrawl
attracting so little attention
a marathon of pages has gotten lost.

Said the Parakeet

B. D. was a decent
poet but difficult
to define or for himself to self-divine,
a follower, a "gift" the way one seeker,
loose but selective,
identified himself
to an intoxication
reading obnubilating poems
in a brick-and-river town:
a generous, ecstatic overnight.
A present, or an absence
needing to be present, who tailed me,
who mailed women years ago when he
was free with his attention,
a fixation that he felt attended *him*.

Sometimes several times a week
then several times a day
he'd write me, for he was free
to borrow books, go to the mailbox
at 3 a.m., for it was urgent that he send
a bride issue of *Vogue, Bazaar*,
(not *Seventeen*, but *Glamour*, but not *Ms.*)
from the Heartland where
(*Don't forget our wedding date!*)
he bubble-wrapped some trinkets, snapshots—
poses of his parakeet beside his own long head

meeting at an angle in a steely mirror.
His wife, from her wheelchair,

had made their camera flash.
He tried to kill his wife
with a little hammer,
the D.A. calling said. The D.A. asks
who are his friends; he cannot name
or call a single one. Define what
friendship saves your isolation from.
Detained, he clarifies for me:
"It was a little *hammer."*

     His cursive changed to printing
turns to scribbling
before during after in the medical facility.
He isn't a bad poet. *A decent poet*
and a bad carpenter, says Vonnegut
at dinner one free-and-easy evening in our town.
Some centuries go by
and on archival acid-free papyrus
or newfound stock of eco-friendly mulberry

     an American *Greek Anthology*:
a poem by B. D.,
and next to him one by Anonymous
influenced by somebody who influenced
anxiety in all of us.
My fragment says, *She lived, who was his nail.*
And she *lived, unguarded, curiously*
—by no one that she really knew—
held very dear.

TWO

Foraging for Sound

I clear my throat: the whole ocean
trains toward the man miniaturizing
            its bellow on cassette. Not much
warning for a rogue wave—but at least my
            interpolation doesn't spoil
his foraging for sound. *Unh-hum* means the
            sea's a big bureau, each breaker
a drawer, pulled forward, of hankies and starched
            tatting, foam's lacy refills, loose
threads that fizz. Hiccups of shells, sneezes of
            logs audition. But what wins: a
whoosh then a *hush*. At ebb, an ad-lib kiss.

Simple Science

Our first time, I was not taking field notes.
The gift was too great to jot down.
Then together for years we bothered
wild terrain to botanize or bug.
When he watered the columned grape arbor
in his life's last hour
I didn't see the Higher Power
hieroglyph his fate in the mist.

It is long past the season of the notebook
and the prosody of the alpenstock.
Too late to scribe with my eye
the scrub-jay fishing from a stone,
to muffle *look, look* and grip
my husband's wrist

with my left that can't write.
The scribbler on some occasions
is a cloud, and, too, a corpulent eraser.
Beware of muddy, grassy diaries.
They'll entrap the snoop's boots
bent on finding wonders
in those writingfields:
owl-shat moon-bones, dark fountains of ants,
a harebell nodding as if reading.

Runneth Over

After the end of his last class in the prison, the teacher saw, and always saw thereafter, shadow-bars across his way to light. Kickstand loved him, and Kickstand could love. Kickstand was getting out, taking his love to freedom. My husband hoped I'd find someone beyond him if he died. He did die. Riding the carousel we had traveled far but never any further now. Golden poles, legs-in-air mares, steeds moored in a painted herd. I thought I'd found *the* map for any road closure or detour. Frivolous map: it was circular, like a grit-sanding disc. I stopped sinning and spinning precisely at nine one morning when I found him stilled. Kickstand won green freedom and the ability to write long inspiring lines. Walter went to feed the darning-needle roots of a small commemorative tree. I held out my best cup, and, for days, the sun wouldn't pour. Until the first beam of sun was caught serving, violating its parole...

The Larry Shirts

Once, when the whole walkable hot flat town of Esparto
Held its annual yard sale, in one garage
A rack of Larry shirts,

Not a designer famous for poverty fashion,
Not a brand sported by people
Not named Hilfiger or Yves St. Larry,

Its color was a dirty oil-green
With an oval patch cartouche crying "Larry,"
Or embroidered script above a pocket.

We grabbed so many, Larry's wife
Looked at us strange, but "Larry won't be coming back
For a long time," she said in salesmanship.

We seized so many it became a mission
To visit friends, with a gift to each
Of Larry's identity,

While he wore whatever blue or orange or broad stripes
Are big in Folsom, Vacaville, San Quentin,
Wherever he moved.

There were twenty-some. And all of our friends
And several strangers wanted to become Larry,
The worker, and if only he'd dealt in Larryness

Instead of drugs he'd be happy too, only too happy,
To wear his name
Made friendlier from his given aloof Lawrence.

Speech Crush

        ...who spoke late
echolalic, then in similes,
by the lake,
where the sticks were her
long mosquitoes, her lava
pyramid brown rice.
        Got a crush on a suffix,
giggled, blushed,
at every *-tion*. And there were
many, in conversation,
flirting with her.
Pre-dejection.
Pseudoabstraction.
        As she grew into
orchestration, a white
sportcoat and a pink
carnation, crenellation,
inhalation—
had I known
too much lamentation?
        I, who have lived
isolation, seen sun
as lion,
its mane's
diffusion; offered her
a turnip moon,
close-shaven.
Parental anomaly,
weird shared ions.
A word-prescription.

A nerve-ending infatuation.
        I'm blessed
she's the termination of me,
last blood relation.
Daughter, if you follow land
to its suffix, there's *ocean*,
which I know your toes,
bare, still-growing, slim,
will never *shun*.

A Quaver

A word would start then restart its startle.
This means the owl, but reminds me of how
you talked too. *Wh-why*? You deduced it was
harmonica lessons, you learned to play its tunes
before you spoke. Your phone messages breathe—
those I've saved—urgently, or haltingly, spring
off, look down, and swoop. Your superpower is
to have no sense of smell and therefore
quickly make a dinner of a skunk.

Be-Bebop is spelling the chord out, breathes Bobby
Hutcherson, *with tri-triplet fluctuations.*
It's not a stutter but a sincere concertina.
The tongues of owls see skunk skunk, stripes
on stripes, glide the airwaves with *breath breath,*
and and, right turn right. "I start with a burst of words,
then I need to pause for half a bar of air."
Air is a steal. *I, I*—pausing for earshot—*I owl,*

owl bear down on the flown-over, slavered-for
hare hare—so dear to talons—outcry of a nipped flare.
Reverse whistle, moist mouth drawing through
its tough horn of a beak, across an orchid tongue
wearing a solo garnet spot—like a coreopsis blade—
as if it had sucked on a lozenge. The owl
relishes the rush it takes to cast a spell, a spelling—
hungering for more—more: *Cre-create.*

Mad Boy in the Odorscape: Sutter Psych Hospital

New jar of honey
Cat's territory
Fish guts under a pier

Clove—the jacks of spice
Salt air over the dunes—it can reach much further in
New leather shoes

French fries at the boardwalk
Hills of manure and barn of hay
Sourdough baking—

but not for ourselves alone
The shoulders of a friend with no
top lying in the sun

Wet wool   wet paint
Pizza   Vanilla
Good skunky pot

Wicked coffee
In the outside world Dorothy walks by
wearing Estée Lauder

Soap on someone
in the snow   Daphne odora
Silver sperm like pitch

around its tree
What a cat knows
about catnip   See Valéry

And missing them, not
knowing what he missed,
made him go

mad
Orange tree in bloom
Cedar, lumber

Winter woodsmoke
Match-head between
thumb and index

If you could smell
these things you'd know
who you are

(I want to tell him)

Since—stripped—you can't
you've learned
the nature of God

a god who turns up his nose

My Daughter Visits Me at High Camp, Placer County, on My Fifty-Second Birthday

Her blind friend lets the air out of her tires because she will not sleep
    with him.

Up here there's not much driving; I don't and there's not a real road. We're
    pulled up here on cables.

No trees with leaves; the biggest most overhead presences grow exclusively
    through needles.

Underneath, scads of tiny foliage Walter calls "guts" prop up ground-snug
    medleys of cold-night flowers.

I attach Phoebe to a red castilleja: *Wherever you see one you'll remember
    this*. She recognizes one later on a T-shirt.

Bluebirds hop the rubbly batholith, keep track of good mates. An uprising of
    drinking-straw snow-plants fences the thaw's fringe—crisp, fragile,
    but "breaking" into water.

Everything I do is fifty-two. My daughter says her poverty rests for the day
    below and west in her sooty city.

I still want thinking eyes. With thinking eyes you can see the new emotions
    that appear, undescribed, all over the flat old ones.

Phoebe's a fixer: oversees a needy thing with an eye to righting it. But this
    is new to her, to wonder about summits.

That goes for small but not yet downtrodden things too, the vociferous
    blue-violet phacelia ankle-alpine and so ticklish it would seal up

forever if she didn't—even on introduction, not knowing she cared—tiptoe
    around it to help it persist.

Mères à nu

I never saw my mother
Even half-stripped—
Now I won't even expose her name.
There'd never have been disgust, on my part, if I could have
Caught her right down to the flesh around her heart.
But my friend Andrea says
Her mother skipped around her house, naked and free.
I'm covetous of Andrea's advantage—
A mother in her entirety.

It's painful to watch a woman pinned
To a self-restraining order.
Stiff-upper-lip Lemon Law, leggy though she was.
(I was the shorter adoptive.)
What could my eyes have fallen
Upon? What lettered cups?
How does one know her own body
Curbed by forced engirdlement—
Goose-beak garters, thigh-high stockings, under-
Version of men's suspenders?

Unnaked mothers—one confessed
Her husband never caught her raw:
Four kids, all those dress-up anniversaries.
Myself, I'm never too old to be seen, to show
My seed who outgrew her place within.
Once we posed together for the Pentax—
Flaunting our long hair—the extent of
Our veil, our drapery.
So what if a belly looks like a radio's concentric

AM / FM rings, a clash of different musics?
Or like a washed-away sand castle?

Better those likenesses than a pencil skirt and wringing waistband.
Not a pretty picture but a real picture, precise as features
On the moon. There are twelve Hasselblads on the flesh of the moon,
On shuttery Mare Imbrium, Lake of Fear, Bay of Dew.
The sun highlights them. Catena Brigitte. Our Bardot
In the sky forever.
Now, my father:
He never said more than he thought he saw.
When he died he only said, "It's hard."
He only wore the hospital gown.

Except he's wearing still
That simple swimsuit
He sported when I was young and blithely burning
In the ocean sun.
She too was there, her thighs, her long arms, her one-piece:
Enough suggestion
For the man who held my naked mother.

Forgiveness is giving up all hope of having had a better past.

—Anne Lamott

Mom is happier before I have a past.
Mom isn't always happy within my past.
She had a tragic childhood.
How long can you long for babies?
My adopted kitten was extra-long, enough for two.
The old fields of our valley—prune
and tomato, onion and apricot—were fertile.

Skeins of chartreuse floss I bought
for her embroidery hobby, looped in her lap,
next to pencilled hollyhock where pickets will be
sharpened in silk. Mom isn't giddy back then.
Her threadless cottage waits for white-on-white.
Not unlike how I hide my sin.
How badly she wants one. But carrying her boy
isn't godgiven yet. Summer shade
will give birth to her forgiven.

Quicksilver, Cougars, and Quartz

> Nothing has a stronger influence psychologically
> on their environment and especially on their children
> than the unlived life of the parent.
> —Carl Jung

i.

She let me have her secret:
The only way to be happy is to conform.
Maybe I seemed unhappy—
So she told me that.
And in return I gave her
Hobbies and obsessions,
Engagements, absorptions, quests, and play.
I never mewled
But came across as uncompliant,
Rebel but not whimperer.
Suspicious to want clothes skimpier.
Seams of a swim suit
Filled with basalt and quartz and feldspar
From the rowdy ocean floor.
Scrolls of waves re-write a swimmer.

The only way to be happy is to conform.

The buoyant water, bubbly on its own:
Water is itself the child
Of water.
Water does it well: happily conform,
Steer supple sounds through watersheds,
All forms of shores, courses, and beds.

ii.

She bought me the matching cover-up.
We will pick you up
(Yes, really they would)
Out of the gutter—
But oh my gutter...! A scape, a panorama,
Of quicksilver, cougars, and quartz—
Their touches, gleams, perches, and glows
No hedonist, no worrywart
Ever worried about.

Quicksilver, cougars, and quartz—

We played with mercury in a box lid,
From our grandfather's cinnabar mine.
Beads of mirror nobody said was poison.
A sport of rolling mirrors.
We could see ourselves convex in them,
Where, in a miner's cottage,
A puma occupied a shingly attic,
A surprise idea.

Visitor or resident?
Thirsty being
Come down from hills to lap and sip, as wildly as it could.

iii.

One day I tripped across, stubbed barefoot,
A prism in a purling, scrappy creek—
Our claim to open water.
A near-dry chaparral gutter.
We will pick you up out of the gutter—

Chute scintillating like quicksilver, tongued by mountain lion,
Lit with washed-to-the-surface crystals.

She meant, Do not vary so much, so far.
I can't go where you are, she must have meant,
When she said
(It will not leave my head),
I wish you were dead.
I wish you were alive.
I wish you were dead.

But not extinct, she could have qualified.
"In rugged, forested lands a rare gastropod":
I wish she wished I were a fossil.
Somehow I felt it made one individual:
To wander off alone, and dazzled.
There still is hope to make her happy,
Afterliving if she is, when I wade across.

Lute Frets Ghazal

"If a lute-player has lived eighty years, he has surely spent sixty years tuning."
    —Matheson, c. 1720

I don't even know a lute personally
but I associate each pluck with a person.

No pocket to carry my pen
on my nakedness. I'll just have to remember.

Birds' euphoria; Mom's dysthymia;
tree crowns, wiggle-room for roots.

I ruined everyone's privacy, thought the moon.
Even a choir's? Even its own iron core's?

Sole-prints in the lazuli just-latexed floor;
she's figured the twist to the knob on the bedroom door.

Flower Moon: first full in May.
If it were a motion-light, would it brighten at the flight of an owl?

Delius was buried at night, with owls hooting.
A false owl on an upper balcony never moves, has no throat.

A huge ache, a mute moan, a sudden showing up—
and we met seldom.

Elizabeth's letters say I had such a hard life;
I did—a hard life in a meadow.

You Get a Free Shadow Along with Me

It's scissored out of shoebox cardboard.
Dogging my heels it protests I tether it.

Its template is the orchard blurred with smudge pots.
It was blossoms, but settled for ticky-tacky.

Alone, it scans the builders' scaffolding. Empty—it's Sunday.
How far down would workmen's shade fall on weekdays?

It's free, just a souvenir.
The waggy tush-end of being.

When we glance quickly up from our shadow,
We try not to faint.

The shape of my mind is an open book—twenty of them.
Also a tailormade nimbostratus. Unilluminated area. Interceptor of light.

Your freebie, my promotion:
The catkin's comet's shutter. I feel you reach right through it.

Coupleting Discretely

I feel Samurai: I spend my whole day sharpening my edge
And then I hear from you and I slit nothing, melted.

1962: My fingers froze on "Indian Love Song";
Then Ethel Waters took the stage in the scented depth of seaside evergreens.

Nights of basketball: every little effing two points.
But if he won, they'd dance in the living room.

One of my lives came to its incompletion.
No matter how many earrings I say I have, divide by two.

What's the guitar equivalent of black keys?
Hand on a D-flat chord: relief map, where the hills start the mountains.

Wish me a feminine ending.
Go out to dinner with a ballad: oh let's scarf up
A slain knight.

One good line about one raindrop:
Wish me an epic.

I've earned a relationship with the involuntary.
But it can't possibly love what I love, and what (on earth, if it is) is "it"?

What is what is "good"? What is "burnt to the waterline"
For a ship off the desert?

I had a gardener worked after his war.
Terrified to step indoors, he banished every black widow from the shed.

For Little Charlie & The Nightcats, on St. Cecilia's Day

("Music shall untune the sky!")

The old van, poor animal, is hit by a deer;
St. Cecilia is beheaded by a sword.

Twelve eyes stinging from smoke off singing;
We are headed towards the fires now,

As we climb a huge grade from NC into Tennessee.
We're in the Smoky Mountains, it is pouring

buckets, cars hydroplaning—we are 30 minutes
from the flames. "From harmony, from heavenly harmony"—

In the thick of things. In too-tight patent leather shoes.
She was "cold, and hot, and moist, and dry"

For Dryden, fast-writing semi-saint
Never in a van with monster guitar-heroes.

Car-misers, you think St. C would die for this?
Smelly men telling the same old stories;

"The diapason closing full in Man."
You worry you'll be robbed;

But it's written music that robs music
If you have to look at it, eyes not on the road,

The road that rises to meet martyrs,
Animals with wild golden irises.

Patron saint of live *solos skittering on the edge,*
where one wrong note will bring the whole thing crashing down...

But it's the right note, steering to get there: airbags
Are bagpipes, hares skid under tires, and owls'

Brows stare into your tear-dusty windshield.
Your life gets siphoned slowly out of you till one day

Her body's found incorrupt, seeming to be asleep—
It's all in the execution. Then, she's up on her feet, clapping

To the chorded shell, the trees unrooted.
With a few of our arpeggios thrown in. Cecilia, the saintly

Hitchhiker: the band swerves her down the road
And right into the camp on fire where the gypsies play.

Upon Your DNA

You claim to have been in this room.
I'll look for you—for it:
Neither wet nor dry, but airy—
There must be a way
It shows your face,

Has a shoe size.
I'll know it when I'm near it
By the sequence of feelings.
It's determined, your DNA,
And so am I.

Thank you for leaving it behind
Yet taking with you more to give next time.
I've found one steel-gray hair
Breathing.
Resuscitated it

Although
I'm sure you keep spares.
Everyplace I traveled there was DNA
I wanted to collect,
But just couldn't

Carry it all, so didn't—
Maybe because of the *snap*
I could hear coming along the vine
Of its helix.
Loopy

Is the quality I like.
I hope yours has it.
Actual scientists
Are not embarrassed to say
Sticky.

Archaic Rayon Kamehameha

for my dad and Rilke

Blue eyes like dusty Santa Rosa plums,
And his fabulous head
In Santa Rosa
Rested.

I put a shirt on that remembered torso
And there's no place it does not see me
From across the room—.
I'm its heiress.

He kept a Scottie dog candle, never lit.
Chenille letters he'd lettered in, *restrained and shining.*
Loins prudent, never shown. Almost didn't procreate.
But once, the telltale cadence of that double bed.

At the end he told me, *Change your life,*
We always do what we must. And never, never...hesitate!

Choro for a Father Dancing

> The whiskey on your breath
> Could make a small boy dizzy;
> But I hung on like death:
> Such waltzing was not not easy.
> —Theodore Roethke, "My Papa's Waltz"

What kind of music
Played for pickled Otto Roethke?
Sound coming forth from what?
Off what needle laboring?

Or did we hear a radio?
My father raised me to dance from overhead,
Not touching carpet.
Yes, there were pans and pots

But Mother lacked a flair for cooking.
No wine goblet to be found.
Dad's nose had been broken
More than once, in competitions

That he won. Belts or buckles,
Chaps or straps of leather? No danger
Except in art, the way it takes church over.
Chairs' toes tap. Gymnastics

Make a small girl stronger,
For, when jumpy and younger,
Soles learn to balance—
On those knuckles he liked to crack.

I ate birdlike, so far weighed little—
Tico-Tico, sparrow in the cornmeal,
Rufous-collared in the bran:
To the tempo of his favorite jazz, we sweated Latin.

Chorus: Canary in the granary.
Chocorado in fields of dry rice.
Tossed to his mimicking—the whistle
Of a red fruit-crow—off I flew.

Birth Mother,

19, sunsuit.
The shadow

of the Nehi
covers her

navel.
The orange

in black and white
flavors the throat

down to the amnion.
Father's grape

forward, corner,
he loved

a camera.
I separated soon

howled pale
until

we all blushed
exactly

nine months
to the giveaway day.

Current, Matadero Creek

Down there would have been my mother,
under the swags of vines,
wading through flats of light.

Prickly, linty tanoak leaves. Minnowy navigation
maternal eyes could see.
Threatened red-legged pocket frog.

Willow. Stiff bay. A doe caught wet-hoofed
on a camera manned only by night.
Missing mother combing for watercress.

Time is a river without banks,
says Chagall. Maybe, she's thinking;
maybe she's thinking...

Mats of peppery greens, stony shallows,
while up on the topsoil pepper pinks the trees—
neither native, both adoptees.

Buson says it another way:
It doesn't go on from here...
The narrow path ends

in the water parsley...
No slovenly, apathetic puddles for us, Motherwater.
I'm specimen of your current. And don't we

get stranger as we let the familiar go?

THREE

Henry, Praying: Sutter Psych Hospital

Keeping this chair beside him—
three times our day.
And at midnight,

when the Cosmos
reduces us to snacks,
still he prays.

Mercy on tiptoes
trips into his ruthless world.
He's formal, a stately murmurer,

with the longest band of gratitudes
even though he must be starved. And even

though he's starving, he
manages a stony
ascending trail of thank-goodness-for-this, thank-heaven-for-that.

Esses whisper where teeth used to be.
No piped-in music, palliative or reverent,
mistimes Henry's peace

before our viands, a hospital class act,
roast *au jus*, not as tough to a springy knife
as guys he knows from the street. Vegetables bright verde,
blues swirled into yellows,

squash in its home of amber rind, pallid glory
of a baked underground staple.

Eyelids down, ropy strands of gray-brown-gray hair,
face washed with grace,
Henry begins to eat
only after he's spared nothing.

I am full; I pray Henry wants my roll and milk and butter.
That prayer is answered.

I remain there,
with Henry's prayer in the air:
something fair's been given him.

(You, God, don't you dare
walk out on Henry's prayer.)

Women's Wing: Sutter Psych Hospital

One side of the corridor is chilly, the blankets lean;
the opposite, chili-hot.
No comfort zone, and we worry about Coral,
here because she set herself on fire.
To myself I call her *Sunset*,
not to dissent from daylight, but to appreciate how
her rose streaks band our evening.
Her forearms: fire arms.
Red muscle diagrams.
That part of our shared body swells,
lathed like a mending egg.
Healing slides new skin like stockings over it.
Sunset reflects on a dull dim butter knife.
The officers who came to me
confiscated my flat scratched one
and my Swiss Grosbeak nail cutters.
They seized Coral's matches.
They left us our emery boards and spoons.
What torments you? What is the threat to you?
Doctors stand behind our defenses cattle-like,
herded together, twilight in their eyes.
We accept dusk's seconds,
changing airs and dances,
flares and chance recognizable cloud.
Do you hear voices?—they ask us daily.
But, no one *hears* the sunset.
No one hears it cry.
Tomorrow morning, ardent and balsamic,
in our women's wing,
Coral will rise when we do,

both ends of the candle
fuse us into a single day:
Sunset will rise with our cry.

Courbet is a Desperate Man

Did I know him? Yes his speed
(did I tell on him, turn him in?)
fell out of his pocket climbing up
my two-story steps—hmmm,
what is this? crystal-like, kitcheny,
condiment no wonder he talked
so fast, eyes switching back & forth,
if I sat at his feet with some slow
narrative. He was a chef—an excuse.

Did I go to the porn shop with him?
Yes, I did. It was the Multnomah
County library gone buff.
I truly loved Naked Mole Rats,
matriarchal and colonial, in the zoo.
Bodies like cherry tapioca pudding
or something more gourmet for him.
Did anyone there look at me? Of course
not. He had said they wouldn't.
I wouldn't carry the bagsful of DVDs he bought.

Did he break through my fence,
steal my fossil stepping stones & Buddha?
Yes, he did. Did he stand the grandmother
clock up in the middle of a room of shoes
to see if it would fall? He did. Did he bang
on my front door at four a.m. to say
his girlfriend wanted a menage? He did,
knew French. Did he pawn my coyote

skull? Yes, even that. Rings & watches
weren't enough.

He will be desperate looking for
"The Origin of the World" from me.
He even got lost in my closet,
having found his drugs. Shameless,
he liked saying where he worked
All the pussy belongs to me.
I wouldn't have kept him
even if he'd liked my cats,
the two I cuddled with,
Dr. Jesus and his closest enemy, Plumie.

Spleenless from Vietnam, he misplaced
his wallet, phone, lost his esophagus. Strewing
lentils wall to wall, he traded
a hundred pairs of salt and pepper
shakers for more meth
and lit the stove on fire.
He was—not quite—panicky
when I grabbed his key.

But I wasn't being rash:
tweaking where I couldn't see, verbose
and orbiting, he rushed about
washing, stuffing the Maytags
with loads from garage through study
into laundry room, bleaching blues,
the desperate dryer tumbling, rolling on
all night, cycling chef coats and poet shirts,
somersaulting dryer with its heat burned out.

Sonnet Composed in Disturbance

After a year I asked Chef who his other clients were.
Oh you're the only one, he said.
He never seduced others with food.
He brought capons & some chichi kind of duck
& crumbled fresh flageolet. No one
for me to be jealous of. Juggling baskets of fruit:
Watch out for the mockingbird nest next time.

I should be mocked. I should be flagellated.
Angry burns on his knuckles.
Cleaning the reach-in & throwing the sweepings in his mouth.
Gary's in prison, who pawned your salt & pepper shakers.
Ralph is dead of junk. Neil's OK to visit you in hospital.
"Rutabagas you fuckers: Tell them I had a purpose."
Who ever excelled & when? The stars. Then.

Feeding the Giants

They were embarrassed—he had to put them at ease.
The shy Colossus & the Giantess had never met.
Persian vines, stamped plum or citron, clothed the oval table.
I sense they didn't trust him. Already I don't.
Tactile breeze on their moist blind-date features.
There was an attraction, rising mid-air near the ceiling fan
(or lobster fantail). As he sometimes overdid in my home, Chef
staged rabbits & feathers, stones & aloe, for a centerpiece.

Chef bragged to them he'd rolled nude over pages of 600
cookbooks. The pair laughed, reassured, from the man's
wingtip toes up to the nose-guard of her giant-tiny glasses
& tight perm. Their hands were too big, feet meaty, troubled
by finger-food. Flame of fat candles. Artichoke leaves
shrinking into tight interiors. Game hens with hot figs
to pinch off skewers. But to Chef, a grand moment, what a feat!—
just like the time he taught a terrorist to make a torte.

Thirstiness

The sun shone in hot from the south
& Chef lined up soft drinks, mostly for himself.
I was finished with spirits & renounced sugar
as well, staying simple. None of this is
"good" the way good should be. But my mind is on
my artichoke, fruiting among the roses. It enjoys
the dance of baby mantises in its leaves.

Feathery fans of fennel volunteer beneath
the street sign—their life is good. We don't have
to eat much for it to be a feast. One sprout
a mentor for another—blue shadows when the heat
gets too intense. Chef reaches for his orange
soda & swallows fast—oh his moustache
swarms with a thousand ants he didn't see.

Restraint

Before Chef hoodwinked me to drink, he led a ewe astray,
his boss's pet in Montreal: completely soused. She fired him;
he left to go shape pizzas for the Greek shop down the street.
He flung one like a discus & it wrapped about that owner's head.
I am his dupe. Officers Trn & Dacanay,* force us apart; you guys
make better partners. Please bar him from my premises.
I'll confess to rhyme it: he's been my nemesis.

He stabbed a portrait of me in the center of my face.
That scrap would be my nose; my eyes kept tracking him.
My real body suffered, mocked with a cast & crutches.
All my motion-lights are on. The locks' mutations
now refuse his keys. He tried to run down men in hazmat
suits, convinced they'd come for him. None of his three
kids by three women wish to wangle their dad from me.

Egypt

It was more than an outrage—it was a belly ache,
the fifty-thousand liquor cakes he claimed to sleep
between, in a sort of gulch. When he woke, his last
cent was embezzled from the drunken bank. His manic
story changed: "Why didn't my father love me?"
he cried out. Sometimes that feels like his summary
so I go down to the garden, where the good food starts.

In damp earth I find a flicker's head. Its beak's
ajar. Small things—an eggshell in the laundry,
tea poured in the iron. He finally finds his wallet
in the peanuts. Chef-coat button in the winglike
fern. A blue pumpkin to cook up. Some cash
is left: two crumpled tens crawl through the trash.
On the sill inside, fresh new tomatoes, from Egypt.

Las Hormigas

They so liked breastmilk;
Joanne fell asleep & leaked,
the ants woke up, made the sweet climb.

Others were surprised to find
acidophilus, Soledad cleansing
her inside sex—they made their way

across her ivory sheets while she napped.
Ah, the little guys were rejected
by our sisters. But still, I feel

sad that in my new lodgings there
are no more glossy arrowheads to follow,
sprinkle with baking powder,

make a pretty cayenne path for
over the once-food-strewn
sill (they scent our past).

They can carry
their groceries
bag-free: & ants shop

in the honey cupboard,
thirst
like black hair being washed

in a sink. Car-waxed
black traffic jam—that's
actual jam, strawberry.

Once my curatorial staff.
But let them go on strike.
Those embodiments of intention;

they don't sit around playing
cards; perhaps they never
play, never horse

around. Hard-to-see-in-the-dark
jet numbers
on the radio dial.

Perhaps there is no laughter
in their chasm. Serious:
but they're able to stand up on hind legs—

a darling trick.
I want to give them
a little inkwell. A beachball.

The number of communal legs alone
exceeds the stars
underground.

They could be an orchestra.
A single one looks in the mirror
& sees a note. A quarter note.

So many instincts
massing as one. If I miss one little lover,
do I miss them all?

Investigation in Gray and Gaudy

"What can or ought
the public care
about
the identity
of the portrait?"

said James McNeill.
Did he look down
from neutral heaven
on the dealer wearing
flannel plaid, adjusting

to my denim chair,
to make the arrangement,
pocket my check
in black and smudge and white?
The agents said

they could easily find it
if I had no carbon.
FBI with their silk knots
and sober suiting
just like the famous oil

though on different
body parts.
I could be
Mrs. Whistler,
but I was

the dupe,
eyes lowered,
the menswear pair
noble shadows,
tracking down

the evil and clever
eBay forger (not
the original cormorant-tousled Martinez
I thought I was purchasing
with his true (M) mark

from his 19th-century hand).
Inspectors with their pointed
interrogations—they were way
beyond clues,
who when they left

would form, and be,
long shadows
at each end of day.
Make shapes you might assume
would fall

from mountain goats
in frightening terrain.
They reported answers
they knew all along.
Thigh-high in paintings,

I thought to wade out
with my honest eyes

so little notorious,
from mistaken
tonalists, expressionists,

Society of Six . . .
The crook posed in tartan,
I fine-tuned
to the agents;
he talked ordinary—that was my best judgment.

So what? He warmed, and got richer in,
my denim wingback.
I thought of Anna's
stern profile; and were they
profilers?

And as they shook
my hand goodbye, I said,
Do your wives collect anything?
What do you think?
they implied.

The Exact Shade of Code Grey: Sutter Psych Hospital

What anomalous culture were we,
the thinning pebbles under a river,
or amethyst-black pearls? The shade of code
meant women, a girls' fight
on cold stone cement,

or stainless steel sink, silver
slicked with shad scales, surfaces we shrank from
so that hearing it PA'd
we'd back into shared rooms
we're territorially squeezed to get along in,

like manx-gray cats in factory-ratty
industrial grass. Let the women brawl,
the nicotine-patched princesses, the breast-biters,
and try to fuzz over the trauma
with pewter lavender of a Weimaraner—

coat and eyes paler and more plaintive
than Code Black, warmer
than Code Blue, maybe dappled,
water-spotted, foie gras or pale-pawed mouse,
coded ways, once something in us softens,

of being our angry selves.

Class Act / Art Class: Sutter Psych Hospital

My place is on the washable marmalade urethane divan with her, urine-runny pants-wet artist, yelling run-on at her son:

My art, my art, I have to keep my art.

She clasps the art of Chartres honored with purple Sharpie, leaf-edge green-goldleaf, orange-yellow. Without caution she's the shout, *My art, my art, don't ask me not to use my mind—*

the way Stafford, mild as he presented, ended his poem with a girl breaking "into jagged purple glass."

Her hand hurts; in her grip, a sheaf of rose windows from art class: *Don't ask me not to use my mind—that feels like taking away my art.*

Ornate tracery of psychotherapy. Grandeur fragile and exercised, dyed as light seeps through.

Rose window, Thou art sick.

But aqua, keep running and you won't get caught. Right away.

A nurse arrives to steal a vial of blood: which would you rather keep— your art's carnelian or your blood's ruby?

Hematological

in the lab waiting room

Romeo... They look around—*Romeo?*
Where had he gone? The blood
they needed was in him, but where
was he? Where's Julie to ask?
But we knew when they'd find him
he'd earn a little bruise, hyacinth
and chartreuse, in the elbow's fold.
We fasted for it. Simple procedure,
so we summon you, Romeo. How
the young technician Adam
calls for you. Time will come
he'll substitute silence for your name,
put a halt to this waiting-room game.
Our turn comes all the sooner
with you in absentia. Your needle fear,
for sure. You slink away, curly cornmeal
ball of a man, not red meat.
Sometimes they have to search, try twice,
even more, but go ahead, go through the door;
let them draw what flows in you,
what runs beneath your skin,
Tigris, Euphrates, Tiber, Po, Mississippi.
They circulate back home:
Columbia, Johnson Creek, Crystal Spring,
your own little pint.

Names at Land's End

Tragedy won't get me
with the smoke of the few
molassesy Filipino cigarettes
I lit in graduate school
and snuffed out with pregnancy.
But tobacco ate
Welch, Orlen, Ray, Hip, Mariana, and Leah.
Franz, Harrison, the sweet Door County haiku-gatherer,
Norbert Blei.
Georgia's inbreath and cough.

Vern in his bacon air, heavy ham of a chair.
Good Hugh Duffield's chains of nicotine tainting his paintings.

O'Hara toked all available flavors
but his poetry sounds as if
there's nothing to worry about,
until *the arrow that flieth by day* comes out of nowhere.

Huff drops his Camel and the whole basement goes up,
two lovers burn down,
ashes soaked in ashes.

Mick my snow-melter, alone in Montana, stardust gone.

Paper remains—no sweet driftwood fire on a beach:
Berry tills them into his Kentucky field.

FOUR

Dodge Ridge

None of the believers would think of breaking free
to search the frozen road alone, with firs,
huge, happy, high evergreens indulged in green themes.
The road dares me from that fireplace, those prayers.
Oh the comfort of cold thought...
The road plays its drama as a downslope,
I see. I guess I was seventeen. I *am*, yes.
Snow-crust, trees, tire grooves, meet a girl with hope.

We keep meeting. And I keep pondering—
pure, soiled, grown into an age
beyond which I would sparkle, hard as ice—
how I descended that rough grade without a guide.
I relied on sierra roots.
I had no plan, except an inkling from my crunchy boots.

Five Blind Boys

In the ho-hum
fence-sitter-beige

meeting-and-eating room,
only after everyone

who had suffered enough—
fallen, altar-called—

came forward and was hand-blessed
by the mother pastor, would the blind

singers go on. With their opening notes,
outside in the pines mockingbirds closed their eyes.

Within, social lighting dimmed in harmony.
The congregation looked to see

if they who never watched their watchers back
showed a secret way of reflecting.

There were ears there who didn't feel a voice.
But they might draw with the sweep of a foot.

Thirty years ago, I said after encore, *I saw you sing.*
But we are none of the same boys, he said, defining.

They do not sing anymore. We sing. We are the blind
boys now. And they *are* because

the shout of Brownlee passed young, the steep pitch
of Woodard slid into sleep. And new

blind hard gospellers came to croon here where
no god ever withheld his jazz

but touched their shoulders
to choose his next hands-up

five glorifying
hymn-powered men.

And women, in alabaster dress,
picked up the next shoutable song:

If not two eyes, two wings.

Last Conversations

One conversation, one only, remaining:
It will be that give-and-take
With Larry Littlebird—
Oral listener—
All about eagles, their shoulders,
Ospreys, their plummet,
And frogs, their singing
Scratched by rain's soft claws.

But any of these exchanges will do:
Charlie saying, If you can hum
It you can play it, if you can play at all.
And if not, sing with closed lips to yourself.
Low continuous sound, your refrigerator.
You must not be lonely.
Harold says someone pointed out
Being begins with a hum:
It seems what you are,
You're happy hearing it, I'm happy for you,
For each other, happy.
Hear it in your colloquial throat,
The syllable meaning human.

Or, if not any of these intercourses, then
Jenny and Chloe, who with a shake
And a nod and a wave of an arm
Toward the East say, We are going
And we'll go on your behalf
And we'll carry signs and shout
The last best protest. Cerise and fuchsia
Sisters, ears pointing out.

Or my streetsigns:
Calaveras (our skull's tacit mouth) and Eisenhower—
War, a theft from those who hunger
And are not fed. Not a way of life at all.
Crossed words on a corner pole.
Movers pack me up, extract me
From that conversation.

I've heard a few words—they stay with me,
An earned ear—and yet
Too brief for brooding. Ghost
Of my father, who never said much
But, *Smell the roses for the camera*;
Or when I ask can I retire
He quickly says, *Don't hesitate!*
Any of these exchanges will do,
"Now is the perfect time."
Not "for what?" but stopping it open.
"April Fool," said my favorite Eleanor,
And then she died. "Good night," her son
Tipped his hat at me,
From the top of the stairs, and then he tumbled.
"I love you," I contributed.
And then I buttoned up.

Swimming During Polio

When the normal man in midlife
sighs, assents to sell his fleamarket doll
whose eyes he loved to make blink,

when our Taiwanese new citizen
laughs telling me he delivers mail
to a clothesline of American bras,

when the blind art professor
adopts a cat that must be silky
and specifically ebony,

when the junior high bully shows
his teacher why he acts out mean:
under his lifted shirt, three nipples...

when I'm hit in the spine by a lime
on my way to baste the steelhead,
and in the breast by a bag of the harder
candy bars, nougat and nuts,
we bought to sweeten the frightening kids,
when my longest-living friend's
entire news she couldn't speak
consisted of "this," when I surmised that meant
the soul escaping from her hopeless daughter,

during the fruitless pumping
on the swimmer's back, the way you empty,
one push at a time, an air mattress to pack away,
the lifeguard plum-slick and smelling burnt,

then I dove through chlorine, a thin blade
filleting a trout, got out, slathered
coconut on small thighs, looked up
at the high springboard's terminus,
from which, once winter's harbor
is drained, you might see all that is left
of one soggy squirrel...

When Dr. Sanfilippo immunized my right rear rose,
I bent the needle. That's when Aunt Ruth
with her oil paints, and the neighbor boy,
the chemist's son, sat frozen with polio
on the hot cement by the pool.

Letter Resembling Things

—From my family I came by a miner's wedge
of pink dolomite crystals
and kept it because their translucence
resembles the wolf eel's teeth,
that disintegrating animal we stood before
for hours in the tourist aquarium's
curtained-off and light-failed hollow,
bloodstars climbing
through convivial, uncharismatic algaes
busy blotting out the only other windows.
It was wrong to trap the years in there
while the eels grew senior,
their cheeks ever more agar-agar,
in this pitiless show business.

In a mineral shop I've retreated to,
a boy, Amahl, tends his father's business,
tries to sell me drusy honey-yellow
crusts of adamite, green calcite
windowing from lime-soda feldspar,
crystals closing gates in the earth with glass.
Nothing closes off in heaven,
but there's no place to put things either.
So I buy nothing yet.
Tomorrow I'll try Marty's Fossils,
but today there were picketers
accusing him of Satanism—
"There's no such thing as fossils;
the earth can't be that old."
One struck him in the stomach with her sign;
another attacked his dinosaur bone...

A beat and formal poet says,
"If to die is to move
from the ugliness of this world,
then let it be."
But what becomes of the curious
when they die? Say, those who want to feel
the innerspring comfort of atoms?
And why does no transcendent world
detail itself in either life,
transcribe its mystical congressional record?
You'd think every day's
heavy tax on the ecstatic
should pay for it.

For instance, I heard Marty shout—
"I just want to show you that the earth is beautiful."
I see him as appellant
for all resembling things, exquisite, ugly,
and miraculous,
even for our eel,
her head so soft a crab is cushioned in it.
Advocate even of her bite
(forestalled when it could crush the sharp crab)
which also looks like rose quartz,
beryl with blowzy impurities,
or palest zoisite.

Sitting on a Desk Together at SMU, 1982

A girl moaning: *I don't*
understand
"Wave."

You said, *Maybe*
you should try
selected whitecaps.

I saw, on a flight
to Honolulu, plane-shadow
on whitecaps.

My eye tried them.
Yours could, in its sleep.
Others needn't think of them

as waves
but as scratches
in the furniture,

light wood under stain.
Obscurity stains almost the whole
half-globe,

hemisphere. The wave
was running at something, a sea-wall,
a boundary that even as fallacy hurt

its nose, forehead. It left
bits of horn on the beach.
And you want that girl to pick them up?

There's a bird crowd beachcombing.
Humans love
going to fragments—

it's Greek.
Pocket the pieces, some too small
to fetishize but not to single out

from the grand
current of forgetting.
There's something unclear for us each:

start perhaps with Cynddelw,
a person of long gentle thinking
the colour of breaking day on a deserted sea;

or when it deserts its own, you'll find
a boot—rust and salt leather
to give back, or dance in;

or should you take the liberty to trespass in the middle of that sea,
re-reckon—*men lower nets,*
greedy unconscious *desecrating a grave*;

or you'll start muttering to remains of springy clams,
their umbones *junked rainbows joined by tar,*
and make thin sense of what you collect.

Faced with bounty of krill,
filter less with cerebrum
than baleen.

It's what comes through the foam.
Here's the take-home:
An octopus wears my wallet now.

i.m. John Ashbery (1927-2017)

Double Elegy

"Ships ought not to work for a living."
—Gwen Head, "Barbarossa"

I think you didn't know
that the ship we balanced alongside
(on the dock that seemed slowly to breathe),

sank
with no flotsam to pinpoint
its final heavy

stinking metal,
how many floors down.
(One can only hope its haul of crabs escaped.)

And Brandenberg, Olberding, Schmitt, McPherson, and Bright, crew
gone to the grave of that year's Tani Rae,
Betty B, Berta J, Miss Humbolt, and Sea Toad.

Though it housed *splintered teak, moldy grain, bits of brightwork,*
and you, your orchids;
voiced moans and creaks, and you, arpeggios;

though it ran with rats and you with mink,
we're all denizens of that liquid pain,
where strong ropes floss in and out of sharks' teeth

and fins freely navigate disaster.
What is it I hear,
why from some fathom do I clearly hear

your laughter?
Where I jotted...

> *a consumptive ship,*
> *the Barbarossa,*
> *pumping out basements-worth of water*
> *all day, all dark,*

you enhanced

> *riding high on the huge, continuous surge of its bilge pumps...*
> . . . .
> *bilge water lovely as any fountain*

Though I tried this—not wholly
working, barely making
a living—

> *You could touch its rope*
> *and draw the huge ship near*

you concluded,

> *The thing is, you can move it,*
> *move* them, *those deadweight tons, with the flat of a hand.*

Pointed Question

Do you have hope of heaven? My brother taunts me
as the sun comes out, as the windshield
wipers dry their blades above this worldly
spattered road. *I can't say*—I believe
in likely sylphish beings toeing the air
with pointe shoes. I hope you sense them too.

The power is out, intersections pass us by.
Almost my life passed. Will our velocity
bother that toppled tree blocking the lane ahead,
traffic-wind rustling through its face-down canopy?
His query feels chilly, makes me shiver,
even by this sanctuary, where redwings
crash from their heavenly high life, flash
signals. I'm not driving, I don't drive,
but right at the edge of bliss, I brake.

St. Écrevisse

Before he knew that he'd been condemned—
by the god of test results
and his inordinate faith in the demon
of self-denial—
an unjust end for a prayerful supplicant—our Brother William
recounted a story
in response to "How was your day?":
He had been taking a walk for his health
and the route veered a bit
because a heavy spring shower flooded the sidewalk.
He had to step around a widening current. A tide.
In one of these detours he sensed
he was being watched and looked down—
at a pair of eyes on a mossy-rose crayfish.
It wasn't about to let him pass.
It stood up on its hind legs and raised its arms,
exalted its claws, at worshipful Brother William.
It held there—in reflected flowing clouds.
The way that once
in a thousand pages which I scrawled at night
and released to fly down to scribbled others
(type them or tear them in the morning),
a single one of these sheets wavers then lands
on its edge—vertically!—
and holds there, erect, individual,
amazed, if it could be, by its own agility—
a hair-narrow curvature.
Three minutes!
Devout Brother William agreed
it would be difficult to tell someone.
Make them believe.

He knew: He was threatened by a little life.
I could see him surrender "the road"
to the crustacean.
The sun would come out, shine through
like old cognac.
And the moon would bump my standing draft,
      en pointe I told him,
spilling its satin words flat on their face.
As for the paper sail and the strong-abbed shellfish,
they kept on trading praise.
And we both held our breath, didn't we,
Brother.

Why I Won't Go Back to Hell

> the growth
> the growth
> the smallest green tendril
> growing
>
> the mind has improvised its
> way to cross the rift:
>> — Kenneth A. McClane, "Ship: Perfunctory Note"

I've scuffed up the way back.
I'm non-returnable goods.
I'd rather have sand between my toes than crumbs of macadam.
My tendril feels like a Japanese bridge.
Suspension.
I'm tickled by growing pains.
Hell misrepresented its address.
I trip on grapes sprouting up.
There's no ivy in Hell,
Even if you judge it as slick, glossy, arrogant.
Jasmine tries a takeover.
Hell expels tendrils but ends up missing them.
Jasmine's coup will succeed.
There's a tightrope walker using me.
That's not flame down there, it's envy
Of zauschneria, from up here on the rim.
I hold my psychotherapist safe by her delicate hand.
The butterfly peavine, the pipevine swallowtail—need me to stay up.
I envy jazz—its soloing.
My brain can always use a passion flower.
I really didn't settle into Hell, any more than airports.
I moved out mentally, little by little.

Boy, am I green.

Hurricane Sandy, with tendrils stretching from the mid-Atlantic to the Midwest,
Is seen Oct 29 in a satellite image from NASA.

Lay your finger here, touch there, and it's not so shaky a stretch.
Because I've been given a guitar string
To swing across.
A tendril doesn't backpedal.
A spider silk refuses to grace Perdition.
Hell has no *fine branchlike terminations of peripheral neurons.*
It doesn't recognize my name, or remember it,
But tendrils write me tenderly and irreversibly in cursive.

The Dijon Sky

The Dijon sky,
a little hot on the tongue
(this dog has panted out

to see its evening),
used to feel its reflection
in a field of mustard

when people—
the inedible, the unhunted—
an invasive species, lived

on the edge of country,
which grew into buildings,
blocky, accommodating

city-limit
neighborliness,
now obits, sad newsy

columns of our
poor prosperous
census.

Mustard had assisted,
extended
distances, popped up

under orchards,
followed wiry arm-lengths
of varietals.

And there among it rose
shepherd's purse,
and pedestal rosettes;

foxtail barley in low-watertable ditches,
light-shredding
grazing danger.

Watch out for thistles
mustard dates;
wild radish crowds,

white and pink;
spreads of bee-brassy
Brassica beds.

For development, though,
a building permit's
taped to your door—

and you'll need more.
Eventually across the street
they build a hospital,

first patients
on wan sheets,
meaning to heal,

miss their mustard fields.
Their peppery purpose.
Too late

to let it all go weedy,
as the pavers call it.
Quick

over-shadows of redwings.
Marking the margins,
an egret bypassing.

Ploughs stay awhile,
then more grown-up machines.
Mere bicycles

turn toward the hills.
Blue oaks,
purple sweeps of lupine,

orange poppies—
you wouldn't call these fields
vacant lots.

All this because
my daughter
asks for Dijon

on her hot dog.
There could be acres, miles,
of experience for her,

tires
rolling into bright safe backroads
of natural planting,

wheels picking up petals,
laying them roundly elsewhere
on a big

sunlit seed. This Earth.

Spill

Mr. Hollingshead fell on his violin-playing wrist today. The girls held his hands and feet; the boys came to lift him into a chair. And from the hard chair he was slid onto a cushioned one with wheels, which a med tech unfolded. Black-uniformed medics moved him to a gurney. He's gone now in the ambulance so full of heart. So close and ready when urgencies happen. But maybe Mr. Hollingshead is wondering who he is now—as I remember from tripping backward over a bulldog-thick garden frog into the Redwood Barn's flats of grinning gazanias and accepting fuzzy aster-blue things. Silly, shocking, maybe fatal for his orchestral ambitions, like the other Sundays we'd seen him sport a bowtie and smart white shirt. We were hearing the music rip in two, a bullfrog's croak to keep the melody from turning into stone. The Rearranger, I told myself, we have met him now.

Faith

I learned *God*
When I learned *see*
Spot run.
But I also heard

Redwoods
Talk to their kind,
And at the edge
Of the moist and the dry,

The pines
And manzanitas
Conferred, their deliberation
Neither garbled,

Beyond belief,
Nor past
Keeping
Its word.

Finishing

Bill Matthews said he knew when a poem was finished.
It was like painting a floor, and you painted the floor
until you got to the last corner.
Then you brushed it in.

Henry and I painted a fir floor cobalt blue.
The walls, paper pulled down, scraped, gouges filled,
we swabbed white.
The day we finished,
we closed the door and got in bed.

That was the night our daughter figured
how to turn a doorknob.

Her feet questioned that the floor was complete.

I told the young poet who asked, *How do you know
when a poem is done*? I told her
these parallels of floors.

Well, she said, *did that leave Bill stuck
in a corner? And how did you get to bed
over the wet floor?*

I do not know.
I muffed.
You're right—that wasn't quite true.
There is always more to solve,
like why a carpet, never?
We loved that her feet were blue.

"You don't know where you are but you go home."
— Hip Linkchain, phone conversation, between Utah and Chicago

"The cage is open: you may go."
— Theodore Roethke

NOTES

"For Cindy, Who Cut Her Own Throat: Sutter Psych Hospital": The end of this poem is clarified by Henry Carlile: "To answer your question, I was told that swans make holes in the bottoms of ponds and marshes. Don't know if this is true in fact, or if something else makes them, but I encountered several while duck hunting, and stepped in one once when it was freezing out and the water was partly frozen over on Sauvie Island. I fell, and got soaking wet. Fortunately I had a portable propane space heater in the truck, went back and got it, and managed to stay warm enough to shoot a limit of ducks and geese. We were married then, but you probably don't remember, and I'd forgotten that episode myself." He no longer hunts.

"Coördinates": "The very last of the Zayante people was a woman who lived for many years beside Zayante Creek. When she died in 1934 she was buried somewhere among the giant redwoods...Her grave, like her people, is lost now." Wikipedia, article for "Zayante, California"

"Mad Boy in the Odorscape: Sutter Psych Hospital": Anosmia is the loss of the sense of smell.

"Springforms: Restraint": These are their truly-spelled surnames.

"Five Blind Boys": These are the Five Blind Boys of Mississippi, in a performance in Woodland, CA, May 26, 1994.

"Last Conversations": The "oral listener" epithet was a way to see how, if I understand him correctly, Larry Littlebird sees himself—he emphasizes, when people call him a storyteller, that he feels he is a "listener." From another Native American writer I was taught that there's a tradition that grandparents teach their young ones how to LISTEN. Before you can speak or carry on the oral tradition there seems to be an obligation to learn the art and the humility of listening.

About the Poet

Sandra McPherson has twenty-one prior collections published, including five with Ecco, three with Wesleyan, two with Illinois, one with Ostrakon, and one, *The 5150 Poems*, with Nine Mile Books. Newer work has appeared in *TriQuarterly, Pedestal, Field, Poetry, The Iowa Review, Yale Review, Agni, Ploughshares, Kenyon Review, Ecotone, Cimarron, Nine Mile Magazine, Crazyhorse, Basalt, Cirque, Palette Poetry, Plume, Red Wheelbarrow, Epoch, Willow Springs, Vox Populi, Whitefish, Michigan Quarterly Review*, and *Antioch Review*. She taught for 23 years at the University of California at Davis and 4 years at the Iowa Writers' Workshop. Her collection of 67 African-American improvisational quilts is housed at the University of California at Davis Design Department. She founded Swan Scythe Press. She is adopted, and is the great-grand-niece of Abby Morton Diaz, Plymouth feminist author and abolitionist. She is the mother of a daughter on the autism spectrum. As a grad student at the University of Washington, she met Henry Carlile in Elizabeth Bishop's class and they were married for many years. Her second husband was the late Walter Pavlich (*Sensational Nightingales: Collected Poems of Walter Pavlich*).

GUNPOWDER PRESS
CALIFORNIA POETS SERIES

ଔ

Gatherer's Alphabet
Susan Kelly-DeWitt

ଔ

Our Music
Dennis Schmitz

ଔ

Speech Crush
Sandra McPherson

Printed in the USA
CPSIA information can be obtained
at www.ICGtesting.com
LVHW041554280823
756533LV00006B/219

9 781957 062044